BEING
THERE

*A Pastor at Woodstock
Then, Now, and Tomorrow*

The Rev. Dr. Paul O. Boger, Sr.

Copyright 2009, 2012

All Rights Reserved
Published in the United States
Amazon CreateSpace

Author: Paul O. Boger, Sr.

ISBN: 13:978-1470062828

BEING THERE

A Pastor at Woodstock
Then, Now, and Tomorrow

The Rev. Dr. Paul O. Boger, Sr.

"Know that I am with you and will keep you wherever you go, and will bring you back to this land; for I will not leave you until I have done what I have promised." Then Jacob woke from his sleep and said, "Surely the LORD is in this place—and I did not know it!" And he was afraid, and said, "How awesome is this place! This is none other than the house of God, and this is the gate of heaven." (Genesis 28:15–17 NRSV)

Contents

Acknowledgments

Family

My gratitude goes to my wife, Carolee, for encouraging me to write about my experiences at and reflections on Woodstock. She read and reread every page and was invaluable when it came to putting together the proposal for publication.

I am grateful to my sister, Nancy, brother, Mark, as well as my sister-in-law, Anne, who encouraged me, reviewed my material, and offered helpful suggestions as this book progressed.

Anne Boger deserves special thanks for finding the only existing copy of my 1969 sermon.

And I must not forget my late brother-in-law, Don Jones, for his *Memories Poems & Essays*, which pushed me to put pen to page.

Thanks also to my children: Leanne, Christine, Laura, and Paul, who shared their comments. A special thanks to Leanne who welcomed me for three two-week stands and one three-week stay at her home in Arizona to work on these pages. And to Paul, at whose home I did the final editing and layout with his wise help.

Last, but not least, thanks to Richard Sartore for directing me to Amazon's CreateSpace through which I published this book.

Churches

I am indebted to the Otisville-Mt. Hope Presbyterian Church of Otisville, New York, where I served as pastor from 1967 to 1971. It was while there that Woodstock happened. If I had not been called by that congregation, I would have never ended up at the festival.

My thanks to the Bloomfield Presbyterian Church on the Green (Bloomfield, New Jersey) whose members encouraged and supported my doctoral program that opened many new ways of thinking to me.

And finally, I greatly appreciate the support of The United Presbyterian Church of Cedar Grove, New Jersey, for encouraging me to use my contracted continuing education time to work on and complete this book.

—Paul O. Boger, Sr.

"The Spring"
by
Don Jones

The Wheel of Life...the cycle of seasons.
It is good to be rooted...
but in the proper season...the flower must die...
so that in the early time...the bud will come...
and...we will live again.
Stagnant springs do not sustain life...
they only sicken those who drink from them.
The spring-source must run fresh and clear...
and pour out over our days...and water deep...
our roots...so that we may become...as open...
as a flower...open to the sun...open to the rain...
open to the wind and the bee...but open...
open to life...the pain...and the joy...
that is life.

Foreword

My husband was a pastor at Woodstock. The proof of this could be found under the white tube socks and men's white, linen handkerchiefs in his sock drawer, where he kept his Woodstock staff pass since he took it off on a scorching-hot, humid day in mid-August, 1969. The badge is still in its original clear plastic holder with a pin on the back, pronouncing: An Aquarian Exposition "STAFF PASS." In the upper left corner is the black-and-white iconic illustration of a dove sitting on the head stock of a guitar. In the lower right, a box with a red, capital "C" which probably means clergy or, perhaps, counselor? Below "STAFF PASS" is my husband's handwritten name.

On the twenty-fifth anniversary of Woodstock I proudly wore the badge to work, but my co-workers were not as impressed as I was by it; I think, in part, because they did not understand that my husband was not supposed to be at Woodstock—not at the age of twenty-nine, wearing his clerical collar and polyester jacket purchased from a Haband, Inc. catalog. He was "born mature," his children and I like to laugh, not hedonistic and, certainly, not "groovy."

By the time he was five years old, he knew he wanted to be a minister, a career choice he frequently acted out for his younger siblings by hoisting his bathrobe on backwards to pretend he was wearing an academic-robe-cum-clerical-collar and by distributing cubed Sara Lee pound cake with whatever fruit juice was on hand to simulate Communion. Married to his first wife at the age of twenty-two, by the summer of 1969 he was the balding father of the first three of his four children and the full-time, sole pastor of a church in Otisville, New York. He listened to Mantovani on radio station WPAT while he wrote weekly sermons in his office located in the basement of the manse. He always had faith. He never doubted. He never despaired. He never second-guessed.

And he never should have been at Woodstock. He went because he was invited by the prudent organizers to be part of a small, volunteer group of professional counselors and clergy from the local area to help deal with whatever problems might come with peace, love, and music. True to his disciplined form, he signed up for the first eight hours of the first day thinking he would be the first one to get in, and then he'd get out and get back to family and sermon preparation in plenty of time for Sunday services. When he was handed his staff pass, it was to serve as his ticket into the concert. Unbeknownst to him, however, the badge would serve as his entry not only into the farm at Bethel, New York, but also into "Beth-el," some Hebraic biblical location he knew from his theological education to mean "house of God."

Dictionaries of the Bible inform us that it is the place mentioned in Genesis where the Patriarch, Jacob, fleeing from his brother Esau's wrath, falls asleep on a stone. He has a dream of a ladder stretched between heaven and Earth. On the ladder angels are ascending and descending. God is at the top of the ladder and promises Jacob the land upon which he sleeps. When Jacob awakes he anoints the stone with oil and names the place Beth-el, which in Hebrew means "house of God." To my husband Beth-el is more a state-of-being than a fixed place, and so, for him, Bethel, New York, and Beth-el, "house of God," became one and the same.

He arrived for the first eight hours of Woodstock and did not—could not—leave until nearly four days later when the concert concluded. To this day he believes the Bethel he unexpectedly entered and found at a farm in Bethel, New York, is as much the Beth-el "house of God" as any of the churches he has served, and in some sense, even more so. Both are part of the same moveable feast— a modern day reference to the continuous gathering of the people of God, at any time and at any place, before there were church buildings. His experiences at Woodstock became interwoven with his faith, philosophy, and theology as deeply and richly as any experience from within the walls of the churches he served from his calling in childhood to his retirement.

Carolee Palmiotto Boger (January 15, 2009)

"Three Days of Peace and Music" A 1969 Sermon

I met my wife, Carolee, in 1989, the twentieth anniversary of Woodstock. We married in 1991. She, ten years younger, was more than curious about and interested in my Woodstock experience. She pushed, encouraged, and taunted me about writing of my experience. I procrastinated. She pushed even more. Still, I dragged my feet. In early 2009 she said, "We are coming to the fortieth anniversary; please think about reflecting on your experience." I procrastinated more. But she kept at me like a stinging sand fly, in the middle of my back, at the Jersey Shore, on a hot, steamy day in July.

In early 2009, Carolee handed me some papers and said, "Read this!" Those papers are now the Foreword to this book and provoked me to put fingers to keyboard.

Yes, I was a pastor at Woodstock on the hillside of Max Yatzgur's dairy farm in Sullivan County, New York. It is located in a small town called Bethel near White Lake.

1

It was an awesome place. August 1969. It was like yesterday. After the last musical note sounded, I returned to my pastoral duties. The following Sunday I felt obligated to share my experience with my congregation in sermonic form. After all, they had enabled me to be there. And there were so many misconceptions, falsehoods, and confused understandings about what actually happened on the Yatzgur pastures. So I begin this project with that sermon.

I must confess that at first I could not find the original text in my files and thought it was lost forever. Unbeknownst to me, my sister-in-law, Anne Boger, kept a copy of this sermon these many years. She found it in the attic as my brother, Mark, and she were cleaning it out. When she called me with the news, I was convinced that miracles still happen. Neither she nor I know why she kept that sermon. Anyway, her decision to do so enables it to be reproduced below.

Before you read it, I apologize for the noninclusive, sexist language throughout my words. But that's the way it was prior to and through the '60s. Although we should have, we didn't think of those things back in 1969. In some respects the Woodstock generation helped to change that way of thinking as it was in the vanguard in the quest for women's rights and inclusiveness. I also apologize for the poor construction of the sermon. I was only four years out of the seminary. For two of those years, I served as an assistant pastor at First Presbyterian Church in Greenville, Ohio, and preached only once a month. So when I wrote "Three Days of Peace and Music," I was still green in terms of sermon construction.

With all its warts and imperfections, here is that sermon, exactly as preached at the Otisville-Mt. Hope Presbyterian Church, Otisville, New York, a week following The Aquarian Festival (Woodstock).

******

"THREE DAYS OF PEACE AND MUSIC"
Genesis 28:10–22 and Mark 6:30–-44
A Sermon by Paul O. Boger
August 29, 1969

A sign on a bulletin board read: "Man's main purpose in life is to give rebirth to himself." This thought could be read in a church bulletin or in the Aquarian Festival's news sheets. The thought fits the church as well as the vast majority of people who were gathered at Bethel, New York, last weekend.

The Christian believes that "Man's main purpose in life is to give rebirth to himself."

The five hundred thousand at the festival also believed that "Man's main purpose in life is to give rebirth to himself."

3

Jesus said, "Unless one is born anew, he cannot see the kingdom of God."

As one of seventeen clergymen and counselors in Orange and Sullivan Counties, New York, I offered to give eight hours of my time to the young people gathered at Bethel, New York. As it turned out, I gave thirty-six hours of the most demanding, intense, and tense hours of my life. I became totally immersed in a culture and philosophy of life I had previously only read about. Here I was embedded in a new city of five hundred thousand. In thirty-six hours I had more counseling situations than I will probably have in the next ten years.

The average age of the people in this new city was around eighteen. Their background was predominantly middle to upper class. The city's citizens were children of doctors, lawyers, teachers, ministers, Madison Avenue executives, publishers, and so on. The lower income bracket was hardly in evidence. As many as 70% of the crowd used marijuana. The use of LSD, speed, STP, and other drugs was less but was in evidence. About all we can say about drugs is, it is here to stay, its use is growing every day, there is no immediate solution to the problem, and no group is immune from it.

Straight society, you and I, is not off the hook as far as drugs are concerned. We live in a drug age: our cigarettes, alcohol, caffeine are drugs. Our sleeping tablets, sedatives, and tranquilizers are drugs.

Housewives take drugs to calm themselves down or pep themselves up. Businessmen take drugs to help themselves get through the day. NoDoz is a drug to keep us awake. Ball players take drugs to keep themselves alert and at the peak of their ability. We all have taken over-the-counter drugs for colds and sinus problems: "Warning: do not drive a car or operate heavy machinery while taking these drugs." "Warning: do not exceed more than eight pills in a 24-hour period."

We are a drug society. We take Cope to cope with life. We swallow Vivarin to give ourselves a lift. All our young people have done is upped the dosage. Take Compoz tablets and be a relaxed, more easy to get along with person. Take seven Compoz tablets at one time and you'll go on a trip—"way out man, way out"—and you don't need a prescription or the Mafia to supply you.

Straight society has come to depend on drugs to keep us going, functioning, calm, collected, composed, and efficient.

Dr. Charles C. Edwards, Commissioner, US Food and Drug Administration, in testifying before the Monopoly Subcommittee of the US Senate Small Business Committee, said, "We are a drug culture society. Psychiatrists, sociologists, psychologists all share with us a deep concern that this trend, this attitude, may be one of the causative factors in our drug abuse problem."

Now, how did all this come about?

It came about because of the increasing complexities and stresses of modern society, the postwar discovery of chemicals that allegedly help the average person cope with these stresses and frustrations. The tremendous wave of advertising over the media, especially TV, creating an environment, in which the consumer feels that reaching for a pill, tablet, or capsule is a panacea for all of his ills.

Delbert L. Earisman, writing in the book, Hippies in Our Midst, *tells us that the now generation uses drugs to "...discover what is going on, where the meaning is, and as a result of that dissociate from the goals and standards of ordinary American society" (p. 82, Fortress Press, 1968). Through drugs, the younger generation tells me they are finding themselves; they are being reborn to a deeper awareness of what true life is all about.*

The drug scene is part of a neoreligious way of life, parallels of which can be found in Christianity.

They claim that drugs open one's mind to the way things really are and really can be. I don't deny that drugs can do that, I have had enough psychology and experience with medicine to know how drugs can alter a personality, kill pain, and bring things out which were deeply hidden within the subconscious.

While at the festival, I put the drug question out of my mind and treated everyone I worked with as human beings who were in need of help or advice. I acted no differently than I would with any one of you if you came to my study for counseling.

I found these young people talking more about God than young people do at church camps and conferences. But their talk alone wasn't what hit me—it was the way they acted with everyone around them.

The exposition was on the verge of disaster; we were at the edge, and any little thing could have pushed us into utter chaos. But it never came. It was the greatest outpouring of the human spirit I ever witnessed.

Why? Because somehow these kids have caught onto something in life that sees no rhyme nor reason for pitting man against man.

A young mother who had become separated from her husband and child while walking to the festival came to me in a state of panic. We talked. She calmed down. I found a state trooper who was willing to walk back to the road where she last saw her husband and child. The trooper returned in about two hours and told me they had been reunited about three miles away. About two hours later, into our trailer come the woman, her husband, and child. All they wanted to do was thank me for helping them out.

A young man came into the clergy trailer. He wanted to call home and tell his parents he was OK. He borrowed my pen to jot down some information as he talked to his folks. He hung up, thanked me, and went on his way. About ten minutes later, I discovered my pen had gone with him. I shrugged it off. An hour or so later, who came into the trailer? The young man. He had my pen. He discovered it about half an hour away from the trailer. Turned around and came back. The pen had cost me forty-nine cents.

A young girl came skipping into the trailer. "I found ten dollars on the ground," she said. "Where is lost and found?" I tried to tell her it would probably never be claimed and that she should keep it. She insisted on giving it to me because whoever lost it might need it to get home.

The atmosphere of love, justice, sharing, honesty, concern, and compassion was contagious.

The kids started it. The police caught it, and everyone else seemed to catch it too.

A young trooper and I were chatting when a girl approached him to report her car missing or lost. She really wasn't sure. We went into the trailer to file a report. She said she had left her keys in the ignition because she was afraid they would get lost if she carried them with her.

The trooper said to her, "You kids are too trusting. You trust everyone."

"Isn't that the way it should be?" she asked.

"Yes, but it's not," said the trooper, "If it were, I wouldn't have to wear this gun or have this job."

"Fine," said the girl, "but if we don't start showing complete and utter trust in our fellow humans, who will start? Trust has got to start somewhere. Why not with us?"

"I never thought of it that way," said the trooper. "Maybe you're right. I hope to God you are right. Yeah, you're right." The report was finished and they both left the trailer.

Where are these kids going? To whom will they give their allegiance? The field is ripe for the harvest. Someone is going to come along with a cause around which these kids will rally. Right now they are generally leaderless; their music and ideals hold them together. Yes, drugs hold them together.

Occasionally I'd get far enough along with a kid to ask about the church. As if with one voice, they feel the church has failed society, and they don't want in the church as it has been known to them. I would suggest to them that maybe they have failed the church by dropping out.

The unanimous response to this was: we have to drop out of the church; it wouldn't let us in. To the average church person, we are good-for-nothing. We are worthless fools.

"Why are you here, Reverend?" was the question I was asked countless times. Good question. All I could think of was the time Jesus and his disciples wanted some peace and quiet—wanted to be alone by themselves and they were plagued with five thousand starving men, women, and children. It grew late. It was a lonely place. The people were like sheep without a shepherd. The disciples wanted to send the five thousand away, but Jesus refused to let them do it. He insisted on feeding the five thousand who

sat upon the grass, leaderless. They fed the crowd and had food left over.

We had five hundred thousand to feed on the grassy and muddy hills of Bethel, New York. Bethel is the Hebrew word for House of God. And those who ate were five hundred thousand. They ate and were satisfied.

Unlike Jacob, we weren't dreaming. I could look out over the sea of humanity toward the stage and see two towering towers, like fingers, reaching to heaven. Upon the towers were multicolored lights making luminous pathways down to the crowd and stage.

Jacob awoke from his dream and said, "How awesome is this place! This is none other than the house of God, and this is the gate of heaven" *(Genesis 28:17).*

As a theologian and Biblical student, I try to see things from a God-centered viewpoint. There was a certain kind of hush over Bethel, New York, last Friday, Saturday, and Sunday. God was with us, he kept us, he gave us bread to eat and clothes to wear.

For one brief weekend, a mass of humanity was thrown into the hills of the country. The ground was our floor, the sky our roof, and the rain the test. The wind blew through the trees, and there was peace and music for three days.

I do not excuse or accept the use of drugs. That's a problem we must face and face now. In drugs I see no hope, only despair.

But in the pouring out of the human spirit at Bethel, I see hope. In some way the religious leaders and people of our nation must build bridges to these kids. We must come to accept their dress and music. We must come to understand their language. We must become willing to share and discuss their ideas, openly and honestly. We must open our hearts and try to discover why they use drugs, because only in coming to understand why they use drugs can we ever hope to see them come off of drugs.

The Sullivan County sheriff felt that for one moment a thin thread had bridged the ever-widening generation gap. If we lose contact and fail to communicate with these kids, we've lost the future. We stand to learn from them, and they stand to learn from us.

Believe me when I say these young people will respond. They will help build a bridge between the gap. They will help to build a better world if, if we will open our hearts like the father of the prodigal son opened his. Utter acceptance.

I think this world has great potential now for bringing in peace and justice. I think the church which we have so long called the agent of reconciliation stands a good chance of getting through to the now generation if we recognize the fact that it's a new world with new hopes, ideas, and goals. It's a new generation with which we must work. The old ways are gone and won't work any anymore.

"Man's main purpose in life is to give rebirth to himself." The church believes it, and the now generation believes it. To the church the way to rebirth is Jesus Christ. To the now generation, the way to rebirth is psychedelic drugs.

In some way, with God's help, we will, through dialogue with these kids, all may come to see that in the end Jesus and his philosophy is the only sure way to rebirth. The kids have substituted drugs for God. It rests with us to show them, through love, that God is all that's needed.

******

This was my sole attempt at writing about my experience at Woodstock until Carolee gave me what is now the Foreword to this book. As I reflected on that August 1969 sermon and my life and learning experiences before and since, I realized my initial thoughts about Woodstock had changed greatly over the decades. Not that I deny what I said in the sermon, but the world in which I lived, moved, and breathed had changed. This changing scene caused me to rethink life in light of my experiences through the '40s, '50s, and '60s, to the end of twentieth century, and into the twenty-first. Where I grew up, went to school, became a teen, entered early adulthood, married, became a parent, divorced, remarried, and now push through my seventh decade, shaped how I react, think, believe, and experience life. Let me share a bit of my past that brought me to the present.

Time for a Bio

Rethinking the past as you move into the future is vital to shaping the future into which you step. It goes without saying that I am not the same person today that I was in 1969. I am not the same individual I was in my coming of age years through the 1940s and '50s. Much of my theology has changed, grown, matured. My politics have definitely changed. My views of society, religious practices, or lack thereof, have evolved. Thus, I reevaluated my first and early interpretation of Woodstock, as seen in the sermon, in light of the years that, "like an ever-flowing stream," have come and gone. As I did, Woodstock took on a very different focus for me. As I looked back to the past, with the "eyeglasses" I wear today, I realized that Woodstock means more to me now than it ever did. It was a life-forming experience: then and now.

I was born in St. John's Riverside Hospital, in Yonkers, New York, on October 28, 1940, a pre-WW II baby. I have vague recollections of our first apartment on Lane Street because when I was about three-years-old we moved to Ashburton Avenue directly across the street from the hospital in which I was born.

Here's what I remember of WW II.

I remember Uncle George coming home because his aircraft carrier, *The Intrepid*, had been attacked and damaged by the Japanese and needed to be repaired before returning to duty. He would commandeer my twin bed, and I would sleep on a mattress on the floor. I remember how much fun he was to be around and how sad it was for us to see him return to active duty.

I recall throwing my tin toy toaster and truck (both beyond use) on a pile of scrap metal at a collection station to help the war effort. My mom and dad convinced me that I was helping win the war. Whatever that meant, I believed it without question.

I recollect my father getting deferred from the military three times because of the nature of his work at the Otis Elevator Company. His division made the elevator lifts for aircraft carriers, and it was determined his job was a vital part of the war effort. His brother, my mother's brother, and one of my mother's sister's husband all served in either the navy or army.

I still smell the plastic-like coin purse in which my mother kept her ration coupons. I loved deep-sniffing it.

I see my mother crying while she listened to the radio of the news of President Roosevelt's death. I didn't understand her tears.

I remember something about A-bombs that destroyed two Japanese cities. As a nearly five-year-old, I had no idea what an A-bomb was and wondered if there could be a B-bomb.

I see myself running around the sidewalk in front of 72 Ashburton Avenue banging a wooden spoon on the bottom of a pot as everyone celebrated the end of the war. I had no idea what I was celebrating. That pot remained in my family until the late 1980s.

All these memories are just that, memories without a firm context. They are foggy, misty shadows of things that happened around me which my young four- and five-year-old mind could not fully appreciate, grasp, or understand. Nonetheless, they had a subconscious impact on me and shaped my early years.

When the troops began returning from Europe and the Pacific, we were informed that we would have to move from our apartment because our landlord wanted it for his GI son. My grandfather, who owned two apartment buildings in Yonkers, said he would evict one of his tenants so we could have an apartment. I remember my mom and dad refusing the offer because they said they would never put another family through the anguish and pain they were experiencing. Our Presbyterian church offered the use of the Parish Hall so we would not be on the street.

As providence would have it, just two days before we were to be evicted in early January of 1947, we relocated to a cold-water railroad flat at 133 Morningside Place, 2nd Floor North. We got that apartment because my grandfather knew the landlord. We could have the apartment if my dad agreed to serve as superintendent. He did, we moved in, temporarily, until we could find another place. My mother was the last to leave our "temporary" home in 1993 when she moved in with Carolee and me.

We now resided at 133 Morningside Place, Yonkers, New York. These were my formative years. Baseball in Lennon Park in the summer. Listening to music on 1010 WINS or 77 ABC, with disk jockeys Cousin Brucie and Wolfman Jack, while sitting atop the back of a park bench. Riding my J. C. Higgins bike all over North Yonkers with my buddies and girlfriend. Taking the subway to Yankee Stadium, Polo Grounds, Ebbets Field, or Time Square for a dime. Riding the ferry from Yonkers to Alpine, New Jersey, and back again. Crabbing in the Hudson River. Hoofing it to Tibbetts Brook Park for a swim in the biggest pool I had ever seen. Attending youth group meetings at my church and munching on pizza following meetings at Rickie's Pizzeria. Participating in youth retreats at Denton Lake.

I started my formal education in Public School No. 6 on Ashburton Avenue, but, when we moved to Morningside Place, I transferred to PS No. 9 on Warring Place. I chuckle to think that my most vivid memories of PS 9 are of the annual operettas we did, field day in the school yard, and hiding under my desk and covering my self with a white bedsheet to protect me from an atomic attack by the USSR. Believe it or not, I was convinced this would work, as many did. How innocent—or stupid. Take your pick.

I spent the seventh and eighth grades (1952–53) at Longfellow Junior High School, which was a daily six-mile, round-trip, walk. Here a classmate and I wrote a comedy about the school cafeteria that was presented at an all-school gathering in the auditorium. During this time I attended confirmation classes taught by my pastor, William N. Colwell, which lead to my profession of faith and becoming a member of the Emmanuel Presbyterian Chapel of Yonkers.

I transferred to Gorton High School, a half a mile from my home, for my freshman through senior years (1954–58). Those four years were spent in innocence. We didn't know anything about marijuana; coke came in green bottles; speed was how fast you traveled; and sex was making out with your "steady" but rarely anything more. My high school group's biggest sins were smoking cigarettes, sneaking a kiss from your girlfriend, and an occasional bottle of beer. Talk about innocence. I confess I was, and most of us were. I remained active in church school, choirs, youth group. I assumed the role of leadership in our Westminster Fellowship youth group until graduation from high school. I read Scripture at a major youth rally at Riverside Church in New York. Gave the sermon at the annual Youth Sunday worship service in my church three times. My eye was firmly set on pastoral ministry.

Yes, there were the gangs, the bullies, the peg pants, DA (duck's ass) hairstyle, zoot suits, sidesaddle stitch slacks, poodle skirts, bobby socks, and the like, but you have to tone down the play *Grease* about sixty percent to get the real picture of the '50s.

Our music was doo-wop, R&B (which became rock 'n' roll), and rockabilly. Our idols were Ricky Nelson, Paul Anka, The Everly Brothers, Connie Francis, Teresa Brewer, and a little bit of Pat Boone and his white buck shoes, and TV's *American Bandstand* with Dick Clark. Elvis was unknown in 1954, and by 1956 he was an international sensation. I graduated from Gorton High School in June 1958.

That fall I began my freshman year at Bloomfield College (New Jersey) as a pre-theological student. The years between 1958 and 1962 were calm. As I entered my freshman year, the launch of the USSR's Sputnik in 1957 was still big conversation as it stole the thunder from the US space program. Mantle and Maris challenged Babe Ruth's long-standing home run record. Ike left the presidency. John F. Kennedy succeeded him, defeating Vice President Richard Nixon, whom I supported. Heaven forbid we had a Roman Catholic who would be the pope's puppet in the White House. Do you believe we thought that way? *Do!* That's what worried us, consumed our times, and shaped our thinking.

During my college years, I concentrated on history, philosophy, psychology, and Biblical studies, with a little classical Greek thrown in. I toured the Northeast with the college's choir, singing in churches as one form of exposing our Presbyterian-related institution to the greater church. I directed *Finian's Rainbow* and *Li'l Abner* for the Drama Club. Ran for student council president and lost.

Oh, yes, there was the Cold War, the Berlin Crisis, the arms race, military buildup, Korea. But life went on pretty much undisturbed. Most in the USA were still basking in the sun of victory in WWII and searching for a more prosperous future for themselves and their children.

Then came the interstate highway system, an auto for most families, travel out of the urban centers, and the rise of sprawling suburban communities. Things were beginning to change, but few realized how much change there would be. Small thunder clouds were on the horizon: race, decline in religious expression, civil rights, women's rights.

I went on to McCormick Theological Seminary (Chicago) in September 1962. In October we all were glued to the TV watching President Kennedy talk to the public about the Cuban Missile Crisis, October 18–29. That was a timber-shaking experience that ended well. I took the prescribed curriculum leading to a master of divinity (MDiv) degree and ordination as a minister of Word and Sacrament in the Presbyterian Church (U.S.A.). I got married in January 1963. Had twin girls on December 2, 1963. But eleven days earlier, on November 22, 1963, at 12:30 pm central time, President John F. Kennedy was assassinated and the world began its dizzying spin through the '60s.

Graduating in 1965, I accepted a call to the First Presbyterian Church of Greenville, Ohio, to serve as assistant pastor. Here I was introduced to the Beatles who were storming the teen scene. Things were still relatively quiet even during the Cold War.

In 1967 my family and I moved to serve the Otisville-Mt. Hope Presbyterian Church. From 1967–71, while a pastor at the Otisville, New York, church, I helped start a nursery school and subsequently spent time working with a child/youth psychiatrist with whom I developed some skills in psychotherapeutic technique. This doctor's interest also took him to the county correctional facility where he, and eventually I and others, under his weekly supervision, worked with inmates who had volunteered to enter a program of counseling. It was while at Otisville that Woodstock happened.

On April 15, 1971, we moved to the Bloomfield (New Jersey) Presbyterian Church on the Green. I had returned to my college town. From 1976 to 1989, I served on the college's board of trustees, taught a course in religious traditions in America, and served as college chaplain. I became fully involved in the local church and the greater church, serving on committees, commissions, and as moderator of the Presbytery of Newark in 1980. This is the closest thing we Presbyterians have to a bishop. In fact, the presbytery is the "corporate" bishop, and the moderator chairs the meetings when the body meets.

In 1980 the Bloomfield congregation approved my becoming a candidate for the degree of doctor of ministry (DMin) at McCormick Theological Seminary. This course of study concentrated on exploring pastoral ministry as a practice, such as in medicine or law. Here I learned how to go about practicing my ministry with intentionality, deliberation, and forethought. I received my DMin degree in 1985.

During 1988 I became absorbed with the work of Joseph Campbell who was born in 1904 and died in 1987. He was an American mythologist, writer, and teacher at Sarah Lawrence College in Bronxville, New York. He is best known for his work in comparative mythology and comparative religion. His work is voluminous and deals primarily with the many aspects of the human experience. I was first introduced to him via the PBS production of *The Power of Myth,* hosted by Bill Moyers. I highly recommend it. It originally aired in 1988, a few months after Dr. Campbell's death. His philosophy of life was often summarized by his phrase: "Follow your bliss." I have read most of his works, some more than once, and listened to many of his lectures on audio or video. In retrospect, Woodstock was a kind of "following one's bliss" experience.

So, this is where I come from in writing about my experiences at Woodstock. Nothing happens in a vacuum. Much of my thinking has been influenced by my past experience, education, and readings—whose isn't? So, what follows are the musings and feelings that come out of my formal, and informal, education experience as well as my nearly half a century of practicing ministry. As I said earlier, during the years that have lapsed since Woodstock, my understanding of this event has been rethought in the context of the above.

Now on to Woodstock—that timeless, mystical, musical happening, which occurred in Sullivan County at a place named Bethel. Or was it Beth-el?

Timeless Bethel

The air was heavy with a summery wetness only a mid-August upstate New York morning can bring. I could feel the droplets of humidity filling my lungs as I wearily trudged across the pasture's mucky mud. It was a struggle just keeping my feet in my shoes as the inches-deep mud under them doggedly tried to extricate foot from shoe. Around me were the leftovers of a great movable feast: sleeping bags, sneakers, jackets, paper cups, bags, socks, plastic ground cloths, bits and pieces of discarded food items. Soon I'd be in my car, homeward bound after three-plus days of pounding music, pouring rain, penetrating lightning, piercing thunder, and a population of people too numerous to accurately count.

As my right foot was about to sink again into the mud, my eye caught a glimmering item of gold. I plucked it from of the ground. It was caked with wet earth. I rubbed off what I could, looked at it, and knew someone had lost it, but what was I to do? Go to lost and found? No good. For thirty-six hours, I was "Lost & Found," along with those with whom I worked. Anything that had been lost and not found had been hauled off to who knew where?

I stuffed what I found in my left pocket and trudged on toward my car. It also was encased in a muddy slime from the rain and wind. I slid into the driver's seat, took a deep breath of relief, inserted key in ignition, started the car, gladly turned on the AC, and headed for home, exhausted and dazed by what I had experienced the past three days. It would take time to assimilate it all.

Once home I removed my unearthed goody from my muddy slacks and set it on a tissue on my dresser. It took a couple days of rest before I explored my found treasure in any depth. Picking it up, I took it to the bathroom and, using a damp washcloth, I cleaned off the remaining mud. I had been gifted a windup Bulova watch with a Speidel wristband whose links were plastered with mud. An old toothbrush soon extricated the band from its earthen icing, revealing the watch's rectangular casing and a small, circular second hand dial imbedded in the lower part of its face. I returned to my bedroom.

I held time in my hand. I wound it gently. It still worked. I set the time and placed the watch on top of my dresser.

My festival garments had to be washed. As I placed them in the washer, my hand scraped plastic on the front of a shirt. Oh, yes, my badge. A 3½- by 2¼-inch plastic-sleeved frame with a safety pin secured on its back so accurately described, in the Foreword, by my wife.

Unpinning the tag, I carried it to my bedroom and placed it next to the Bulova.

I was in possession of a watch and a badge. Souvenirs of what has become one of the most remembered and recognized musical event and happening in all of time.

That was yesterday, and many years of yesterdays have passed that yesterday. And until 2010 I housed the Bulova and badge in my dresser. Every time I opened the dresser drawer, that watch and name tag seemed to encourage, if not haunt me, to put Woodstock into a perspective no one else, to my knowledge, has.

Recall, it had several names: "Woodstock Music and Arts Festival," "An Aquarian Exposition," "Three Days of Peace and Music." We know it now as "Woodstock." However, in my pastoral mind, it will always be Bethel, three days of massive humanity, music, peace, tents pitched, sleeping bags soaked, plastic ground cloths, smoky air, mud-caked clothes, and stones for pillows.

Oh, how awesome was that place.

My study of Hebrew reminds me that the word Beth-el is a place—a special, powerful, deeply symbolic and meaningful place. One dictionary of the Bible introduces us to Beth-el:

> Beth'-el [house of God]. A town in Palestine w[est] of Ai, s[outh] of Shiloh and near Michmash. Abraham on his 1st journey into Palestine, and subsequently, pitched his tent near it. The town was called Luz by the Canaanite; but

Jacob called the place close by, where he passed the night sleeping on the ground, Bethel, on account of the vision which he saw there, and he erected a pillar on the spot. (*Westminster Dictionary of the Bible*, Westminster Press, Philadelphia: 1944, p. 68)

The "Three Days of Peace and Music," set for Friday, August 15 through Sunday the seventeenth of 1969, was birthed in Sullivan County's unincorporated hamlet of White Lake, New York.

To be more precise, it was another place named Bethel.

The distinct, instantly recognizable voice of Richie Havens flowed over Bethel's hillside at 5:10 p.m. as he sang "High Flyin' Bird." I was still in this place on August 18, which became the actual closing date, as Jimi Hendrix put the event to rest with his "Hey Joe" at 10:30 a.m. The stage fell silent. The music was gone. The tents were folded. The crowds disbursed. It was over. Silence now flitted over the pasture, but the memories of that place and event still resonate deeply within me and many others. It dawned on me that I had not seen most of the performers on stage, but I heard them. I heard but did not fully see.

Many have wondered what would happen in any city of 450,000-plus people, over eighty hours, if food, water, and sanitary facilities were scarce and thunderstorm rains turned pastureland into mud-land, four inches deep. It

28

would be a recipe for disaster. At Woodstock disaster didn't happen. "Three Days of Peace and Music" did.

Why?

We were in Bethel.

Or was it Beth-el?

I was in my second year as pastor of the Otisville-Mt. Hope Presbyterian Church in Orange County's Otisville, New York. This was the second church I had served, but the first as solo pastor. I was a "wet behind the ears" minister and wouldn't celebrate my twenty-ninth birthday until late October 1969. I was married, the father of twin daughters approaching their sixth birthday and another not yet into her second month.

My study/office was located in the basement of the church manse. When asked by her kindergarten teacher what her father did for a living, one of the twins said, "Daddy gets up in the morning, has some coffee, reads the paper, picks up his Bible, and goes downstairs to the basement."

What a great description of a pastor's work:

Coffee = Sacrament

Newspaper = World/Culture/Cosmos

Bible = God

Basement = symbolic of where many live life.

Yes, from the mouth of babes.

It was a June day in 1969. I was preparing my sermon for the coming Sunday. My high-fidelity radio was tuned to the soft music of the now defunct FM station WPAT

Radio out of Paterson, New Jersey. Yes, I was a Montovani sort of music lover. I had never heard of Santana, John Sebastian, Canned Heat, Credence Clearwater Revival, Janice Joplin, Joe Cocker, and the rest of the deities of the baby boom generation. And just how could there be the Grateful Dead, Sly and the Family Stone, an airplane named Jefferson, Ten Years After, and The Who?

My phone rang. Little did I know answering that call would set me on a journey that would immerse me in one of the most historical musical gathering in history. I was about to be drawn into an awesome, mystical experience.

"Hello, Reverend Boger?"

"Yes," I replied.

I remember the caller saying something like: "I represent Woodstock Ventures, Inc. We are the producers of an upcoming major musical event to be held in Sullivan County, New York. It's called the Woodstock Art and Music Festival. We were planning to have it in Wallkill, New York, but have to move it to Bethel, New York. The producers want to include clergy and counselors as support staff for the event. Are you interested?"

My response was, "Tell me more."

I was given the details and background of the upcoming August event. I agreed to attend a luncheon meeting in Middletown, New York, to discuss what would be my responsibilities if I decided to serve.

On the appointed day, I cruised from Otisville to Middletown on Mt. Hope Road in my '68 blue Chevelle. Soon I found myself at a large table with representatives of the festival's producers and about twenty other clergy and counselors. Sandwiches and beverages were provided.

They briefed us thoroughly on the plans for the event. Its producers wanted to have religious and psychological professionals present to work with people who might need support and help in relation to drug abuse, family concerns, sexual or interpersonal problems, as well as other situations that would need the expertise of crisis intervention folk.

After the presentation a period of questions and answers followed. Then they asked us if we would be interested in signing on for an eight-hour time slot.

I volunteered quickly for the first eight hours on August 15, the event's scheduled opening. I would get in, get it over, get out, and get home to family, church, Sunday plans, and WPAT Radio.

But, other plans where in wait at Bethel in 1969.

Being There: A Pastor at Woodstock, Then, Now, and Tomorrow

Bethel Time: August 1969

June and July went by quickly.

On August 15, 1969, I put on my gray, short-sleeved clerical shirt and, temporally, pinned my official "An Aquarian Exposition" staff pass to my polyester jacket from Haband. Soon badge would be moved to shirt and clerical collar removed to pocket as heat and humidity dictated. I set out about 2:00 p.m. in my blue Chevelle, driving the thirty miles up Route 209 North, to Route 17 West (the Quickway), onto Route 17B into Bethel. It would take me about forty minutes.

I soon realized I was not in a normal traffic pattern when I turned off of 209 onto the Quickway. There were too many cars, vans, station wagons, motorcycles, and old school buses for this time of day. With each passing mile, the congestion worsened. State police directed traffic, which was now bumper-to-bumper. Helicopters flew overhead. Seeing my staff badge, a state trooper allowed me to Exit Route 17 onto 17B toward Bethel. This rural two-lane road was worse than any New York City traffic jam I ever endured. And I had experienced many as a native of Yonkers, New York, which borders NYC.

People and vehicles were everywhere. Folk were walking, hitchhiking, sitting on guardrails, rocks, and grassy areas. Vehicles were on the road, off the road, overheating, parked in the newly created "parking lot" in Sullivan County.

By the time I got to the right turn off of 17B onto Hurd Road leading to the Yatzgur farm, I had kids in my car, on my car, and jogging alongside my car. At one point I had to stop and ask those sitting on the hood to leave a path of vision so I could see where I was going. Directed to a dirt parking field, I parked, turned off the engine, got out, and locked my car. My "passengers" thanked me for the lift with the peace sign and a simple, "Peace, brother."

Oh, yes, speaking of brothers, my brother, Mark, nineteen years old at the time, told me he had tickets long before I knew anything about the event. He started out from Yonkers, New York, on August 15 and never got to Bethel's Woodstock. On the other hand, I, the very proper, clerical collar bedecked, easy music listener, Rev. Paul O. Boger, ten years my brother's senior, had no tickets, only that staff badge as my entrance pass. As of yet, I had no clear understanding of what was in store for me while at these "three days of peace and music." My brother has never forgotten, and is still a bit of envious, that the one who didn't appreciate the music of the '60s got in and the one who thrived on it was left out. It was sort of a "first shall be last and the last first" thing.

As I strolled from my car, I was directed toward a cluster of trailers set up near the stage area. I wound my way in, out, around, and through a cloud of "smoke" wafting over a sea of people sitting or reposing on blankets while they faced the empty stage waiting for the first of their generation's superstars to appear.

I arrived at the trailer compound. It consisted of several units reserved for police, event officials, information, communications, first aid, and counselors/clergy.

The unit out of which I would work was furnished with several small tables, chairs, telephones, pads, and pencils. Folding chairs lined one of the trailer's walls. Near the entrance sat several large plastic trash cans that eventually overflowed with lost items waiting to be found. As I said, when I found the Bulova, we were "Lost & Found." That can be taken in more than one way. However, most of the countless wallets, purses, keys, watches, and various personal items were never retrieved. Neither were the assorted drugs, for fear of possible arrest for drug violations.

The stage was hardly visible from our vantage point. It was more than a good stone's throw away. I never saw, only heard, most of the performers.

Connected to the massive stage, a wooden ramp lead to a helicopter landing pad to fly the performers in and out. As the festival population grew to the size of a city, medical evacuations had to be made from the same pad. Soon most airlifts were flown by US Army medical teams from then Stewart Air Force Base near Newburg, New York. It was ironic that this same military against whom many attending the event usually protested, now chanted, "They are not our enemy."

At least forty-five doctors where brought in to handle "the city's" growing medical needs. I am still of the understanding that all of them volunteered without pay. Not far from the landing pad was a large tent that served as one of the temporary hospitals, with cots, pillows, blankets, and medical supplies. On more than one occasion, I would be summoned to one of the tents to engage confused, sometimes overdosed, young folk.

The producers of the event had thought of everything. Well, almost everything. They never anticipated the tsunami of human beings that broke onto the shore of Yatsgur's dairy farm. Temporary hurricane fences, intended as crowd control, were overthrown and lay like intertwined wire walkways where they fell. No tickets were collected or needed. Everyone who managed to get to Bethel got in. When you think of the developing situation, the only logical crowd control was to not collect tickets

Most of the free phone calls to anywhere, from our trailer, were made by kids who called home to tell mom or dad that they were safe. I mostly heard "I'm okay" followed by "I love you." The news media, as it often does, tried to make things appear worse than they were. That's not to say things were good; they were and they weren't.

The most frequently asked questions of me, when spotted with my clerical-collar bedecked neck, "What are you doing here, man?" "Is that collar for real?" "Are you in costume or something?" "Hey, tell me about that thing you're wearing!" My clerical garb opened many doors, making it easier to confront and be confronted. Most people exhibited a sense of trust toward me when they saw that collar. Often, when learning I was a pastor, the response was, "That's cool, man!"

On one of my visits to a "tent" hospital, a medical doctor asked me to talk to a young woman who recently had an abortion, illegal back then, which had gone bad. Infection had set in, and she was facing certain death, all because she did not want to admit she had had an abortion.

I remember asking her, "Do you want to die?"

Through her pain and tears, she replied, "No, pastor."

"Well, you are going to if you don't tell the doctors the truth and give them permission to treat you."

With the physician by my side, she admitted to the abortion and said she didn't want to go to jail. We promised her she would not have to worry about that, and later she was flown out to a hospital. I often wonder what happened to her.

One young man stumbled up the two steps to enter the trailer where we clergy and counselor types hung-out. His eyes glistened with fear. His body language spoke of despair. "I lost my wallet, I lost my wallet, has anybody turned in my wallet?" he said in exasperation. I told him to sit down, have a Coke, to catch his breath. Once he did, he explained that his wallet had all his money in it as well as his ID and driver's license.

We systematically went through the myriad of wallets that ended up in our "Lost & Found" barrels. His was not among them. He started to become frantic again: "What am I going to do? How will I get home? Who can help me out of this?" I told him to give us his name, to go back to the concert, to check in with us every few hours, and not to worry about getting home; something would work out. He checked in regularly—no wallet.

The next day he showed up at the crack of dawn looking for the lost wallet. As he walked through the trailer door, I stuck out my hand and said, "Here's your wallet!"

He broke into tears and hugged me so hard I thought my ribs would crack as he said, "Thank you, Reverend." I told him not to thank me and how during the night, someone came to our trailer and turned in the wallet with the words, "Some one might need this." The honest stranger disappeared into the darkness. Nothing was missing from the lost, now found, wallet.

A distraught girl came running up to me as I made my way to the Hog Farm Commune. "Father, Father, help me, please." (The clerical collar always gets a "Father." It even happened the night my twin daughters were born in 1963 as I exited the hospital elevator. "Good evening, Father," said the woman. Under my breath I said, "If only she knew how true those words were.") "Father, please help me!"

"What is it?" I asked.

She breathlessly told me the friends with whom she came decided to leave early and didn't tell her. She was going to need a ride to the Pittsburgh, Pennsylvania, area.

Through word of mouth, we were able to get the message of need out. Within an hour she had over twenty-five offers for a ride to western Pennsylvania.

"You guys are far out angels," she told us as she went off with some newfound friends from Pennsylvania.

Three police officers, one local and two state troopers, took refuge in our trailer as the rains gradually became heavier. Their trailer was already filled to the maximum with other law enforcement people seeking refuge. We invited them in from the storm. They sat out of view from the entrance door.

The young folk popped into the trailer with newspaper, plastic, cardboard, or whatever they could find to protect their heads from nature's shower. As they found refuge from the rain, down came the "headgear." It was sort of funny to watch their eyes widen to saucer size when they spied the three lawmen. We'd tell them not to worry; they were just getting out of the rain like everyone else. Each time, one of the officers would assure the surprised, expecting-to-be-busted person or persons to keep cool—no one was going to be arrested. We were all in this together.

The weather turned ugly. A chant washed over the crowd, "No rain, no rain, no rain!" But it came in torrents with wind, lightening, thunder. No one thought of leaving, only of "riding it out." People were warned to stay away from the light towers. The electrical equipment on stage and elsewhere were covered with tarps. Power was lost or turned off for a while, but a peace prevailed in Bethel. The ground underfoot slowly turned into a sea of mud deep enough to suck your feet out of your shoes. Some improvised, turning large pieces of cardboard into sleds used to mud-slide down the hills.

In between the storms, the music went on, peace went on. Joe Cocker sang "With a Little Help from My Friends"; Joan Baez performed her rendition of "Swing Low"; Janice Joplin's unforgettable "Work Me, Lord" shrieked loudly and echoed over Bethel's hills; Ravi Shankar's music filled the air. I thought to myself how strangely peaceful it all seemed though no police were needed. There were no guns and very little trouble.

I looked out of the door of the trailer as another storm struck. With the rain water flowing between the trailers like the rush of the Colorado River rapids, I observed a young man sitting under one of the trailers and seeking refuge from the relentless deluge. The rushing water began to wash away the earth under the jacks upon which the trailer sat for stability. Within seconds the trailer slipped from the supporting jacks, rolled forward, and began to tip. I thought the man under the trailer was doomed. There was no way to get to him in time. As the trailer rolled forward, its hitch tipped toward the ground and dug into the earth like a plow. The hitch must have wedged against a buried rock because the trailer suddenly stopped. The young man rolled over and out from under the trailer with nothing but shattered nerves and mud-drenched clothing.

When the rains stopped, I strolled passed a pond on the farm to discover thirty or more taking their morning bath with no apparent concern for their common nakedness. It was good clean fun and the only way to stay partially clean. There was laughter, water games, heads, and other things, bobbing in and out of the water. It was like an old-time revival tent meeting baptism. Some in the pond invited me to join them. I graciously declined and walked on.

Many infants and children were at Bethel. I still envision them running around partially or fully naked, frolicking in the mud, dancing to the music. Some toddlers were draped around their father or mother's neck as if riding a horse as Mom or Dad jumped up and down to the beat of the music. Other parents held their loved children close, trying to comfort them at the height of the storms. Some had flowers in their hair. All seemed as happy as one could expect youngsters to be under such conditions.

God bless the Hog Farm, a commune from California. They lived on a farm in Sun Land, California, which had been offered to them by its owner. The offer came with the understanding that they would take care of the owner's hogs: thus the name Hog Farm Commune. In 1967 they began to travel to rock concerts in old school buses. They entertained and fed the "audiences." Their name went with them wherever they went. Invited by the producers of Woodstock, they came in their buses to Bethel and offered simple medical care and set up a free food kitchen. On one of my trips to their site, through the rain and mud, I saw one of their leaders, Wavy Gravy (aka: Hugh Romney) and fellow Hog Farmers feeding anyone who came by in need. These folk were no less than a gift or blessing from God. At Bethel they were pivotal in helping to keep a bad situation from deteriorating into chaotic mayhem. How many they fed is unknown. But it reminded me of another feeding of thousands, on another hillside, in another place not far from another Beth-el. I can't say enough about these peace-loving, polite angels of hope who appeared in the midst of potential despair and disaster and helped save the day. They truly were the "Peace Police" as many called them.

The smells of Bethel still linger in my nostrils. The campfires, camp stoves, ozone from the lightning, marijuana, cigarettes, damp clothes, wet, matted, and muddy grass and hay. Sweat.

The sounds of Bethel linger longer. Much to my brother's chagrin, I heard, live, his musical deities: Jimmy Hendrix; Janice Joplin; Joe Cocker; Grateful Dead; Jefferson Airplane; Crosby, Stills, Nash and Young; and many more.

I watched helicopters arrive, descend and ascend. It was like a modern day Jacob's ladder event as recorded in Genesis. Each star would descend, walk the bridge to the stage, perform number after number, and then ascend as gods returning to heaven, from whence they had come, as grateful worshipers sent them off with cheering voices, loud clapping, ready to greet the next deities in the musical pantheon.

Before arriving at Woodstock, the musicians who performed there were just names I had heard, mostly from my brother, or read about in the news. I know who they are now and have come to appreciate their musical messages and the special place they played in the lives of so many, including mine.

The special place they played in my life at Bethel was the experience of being imbedded in a mass of human beings who, with me, were on a life-quest, a search for the meaning of life.

If the reader would like to get a feel for the sounds and sights at Woodstock, I recommend listening to the recording entiled, *Woodstock* by Cotillion/Rhino Company from 2009 and the 1970 documentary film *Woodstock.*

Time, Vision, Myth, Metaphor

In my pastoral opinion, Woodstock became a life-quest at a most critical time in history. Those there, including myself, thought we were searching for a meaning to life, but I know now that what they and I really yearned for was discovering a life of meaning, an experience of being alive.

Proverbs 29:18 (King James Version) says, "...where there is no vision the people perish."

Joseph Campbell, the famed mythologist, said that it is myth that gives life a meaning. I believe a life of meaning, the experience of being alive, can only be discovered as we live our lives in the context of *time, vision, myth,* and *metaphor.*

Now that I am in my seventies, I am more convinced than ever that none of us is really searching for a meaning to life. What in the world does it mean to search for a meaning to life? Is there a meaning to death, a meaning to birth? I have no idea and, to be quite honest, I could care less.

What I am interested in is a life of meaning, the experience of being alive, becoming and being really alive.

Deep down, perhaps subconsciously, we are all on a quest for a life of meaning. We are looking for that experience of being alive. Such a search must be done in the context of an understanding of *time*; discovering a *vision* through which to live; embracing a valid *myth* to serve as the spectacles that put life, the world, and all that is around us into meaningful focus; and adopting a *metaphor* that will enable us to interpret it all.

What does this have to do with my understanding of Woodstock and its impact on the years following it? Everything. Everything. Bear with me as we explore time, vision, myth, and metaphor.

Time

Time is a strange thing. We live with it and can't live without it. Some view time as cyclical where things just keep coming round, coming round, again and again. The concept of reincarnation fits into this understanding quite well. Others define time as linear with a beginning, middle, and ending. Either way, we all live by it, love by it, fight by it, play by it, work by it, sleep by it, cook by it, and grow older by it, and die by it. We all search for a life of meaning and the experience of being alive within the context of time. You just can't get away from time.

The Aquarian Exposition, we now call Woodstock, was couched in time in more than one way. As my

Woodstock Bulova ticks away the days, months, and years, it is forever reminding me that Woodstock was not birthed in a vacuum. It grew out of a myriad of things spinning through time and coming together at a particular time.

In the New Testament, two Greek words are used for our word *time*. One of these words is *chronos*, the other *kairos*.

Chronos Time

From the Greek word *chronos*, we get our word *chronology*—years, months, calendars, clocks, and the steady, predictable tick-tock of watches. It is in Chronos Time where most of us spend the time of our lives. Getting up to go to work, cleaning the house, making dinner, doing our school work, shopping, loving, hating, playing. Tomorrows and tomorrows and tomorrows come and go. The tick-tock, tick-tock of my Bethel Bulova moves us into the future. Chronos is the time that keeps marching on.

Woodstock was a chronos time. It had a beginning, middle, and ending. Yet, it keeps going on and on in a cyclical sort of way as well. One thing is for sure, Woodstock sprung from the time that preceded it.

Earlier I shared my formative years. What about the formative years of those at Woodstock, the '60s?

Think about the chronos, the chronological time frame that preceded this arts and music festival. On

Bethel's hillside, where thousands pitched their tents, laid their heads on rocks for pillows, and sought shelter from the storms, were those who, during their formative years, experienced the events so aptly outlined and recorded by Mike Wright in his book, *What They Didn't Teach You About the 60s*. My wife, Carolee, gave me this well-documented book as a Valentine's gift in 2009 as I was embarking upon the early days of this writing venture. I recommend it to those who are interested in the decade, in which many analysts believe, America lost its innocence and came of age.

I am grateful to Mr. Wright for his book's detailed chronology of the 1960s. I highlight a few of those events which are pertinent to the theme of this book:

Chronology

1960

February 1: When a waitress at a "Whites Only" lunch counter at Woolworth's in Greensboro, North Carolina, refuses to serve African Americans, four students begin a sit-in. The movement quickly spreads to other states...

....November 8: Kennedy-Johnson ticket edges out Nixon-Lodge in election....

....December 20: Ho Chi Minh organizes South Vietnamese communists the National Liberation Front (NLF).

1961

January 3: U.S. breaks off diplomatic relations with Cuba.

January 20: JFK inaugurated president....

....May 4: Freedom Riders test desegregation in South....

....May 14: White mobs in Alabama attack Freedom Riders.

December 11: JFK sends 400 American military personnel to South Vietnam.

1962

....June 11: Students for a Democratic Society (SDS) hold first national convention....

....September 20: James Meredith tries to enroll at Old Miss....

....October 22: Cuban missile crisis.

December 31: More than 11,000 U.S. military personnel are now in South Vietnam.

1963

February 19: Betty Friedan's Feminine Mystique *published.*

April 2: Dr. Martin Luther King Jr. leads Birmingham, Alabama, campaign against segregation; Sheriff Bull Connor sets police dogs on demonstrators....

....August 28: Martin Luther King delivers "I have a dream" speech...

September 15: Bomb kills four African American girls in a Birmingham church....

....November 22: JFK murdered in Dallas; Lyndon Johnson assumes presidency.

November 24: Lee Harvey Oswald murdered in Dallas.

1964

January 8: LBJ declares "unconditional war on poverty in America..."

....June 21: Three Mississippi civil rights workers disappear; their bodies are discovered forty-four days later.

July 2: LBJ signs Civil Rights Act of 1964....

1965

...February 7: LBJ orders bombing raids on North Vietnam.

February 21: Malcolm X assassinated.

March 7: Two hundred police attack civil rights marchers outside Selma, Alabama.

March 8: First American combat troops land in South Vietnam....

....August 11: Thirty-four people die during rioting in Watts section of Los Angeles.

October 15: Upwards of 100,000 demonstrators nationwide protest American involvement in Vietnam War....

1966

....March 24: U.S. Selective Service says college deferments will be based on scholastic performance.

May 16: SNCC (Student Non-violent Coordinating Committee) elects Stokely Carmichael as chairman, shifting emphasis from civil rights to black power.

October 15: Black Panther Party formed.

1967

....January 14: Some 25,000 hippies jam San Francisco's Golden Gate Park for "Be-In."

January 16: In Tuskegee, Alabama, Lucius Amerson is sworn in as the first black Southern sheriff of the 20th Century...

1968

January 1–June 15: National Student Association estimates that 221 major demonstrations at 101 colleges involve some 39,000 students...

....January 31: North Vietnamese and Viet Cong troops use the Tet truce to launch a massive offensive in South Vietnam.

February 8: South Carolina state police kill three students when blacks try to desegregate South Carolina State College in Orangeburg....

....March 16: U.S. troops massacre villagers in My Lai, Vietnam.

March 31: LBJ announces halt of U.S. air and naval bombardment of Vietnam, then says he will not seek another term in office.

April 4: MLK assassinated in Memphis, Tennessee.

May 17: Antiwar protestors break into the draft board office in Maryland.

June 5: Robert Kennedy assassinated....

....August 28: Democrats in Chicago nominate Hubert Humphrey for president as thousands demonstrate outside in "police riot."

November 6: Nixon elected president...

1969
....July 20: U.S. astronauts land on Moon.

August 15: Woodstock Music and Art Fair begins in pasture outside Bethel, N.Y...

....November 15: Some 250,000 anti-Vietnam War demonstrators rally in Washington...

> *....December 4: Chicago police kill Black Panther Party leader Fred Hampton.*
>
> *1970*
> *May 4: Ohio National Guardsmen kill four Kent State University students protesting President Nixon's announced plan to launch a major offensive into Cambodia.* (Mike Wright, *What They Didn't Teach You About the 60s,* Presidio Press, Inc. Novato. California: 2001, p. IX–XIV.)

In the mud and rain at Bethel was encamped a generation whose parents' chronology, or chronos time, was spent being the "greatest generation," as Tom Brokaw baptized them. The parents of those in Bethel saved the world from shear Hitlerian and imperial madness. As chronos time passed, their offspring became unaware of the sacrifices that shaped their parents' lives and gave them a reason for being alive and thus a life of meaning.

Dancing and singing in Bethel was a young generation caught up in the struggle for civil rights and the aftermath of the race riots of 1967.

Smoking and "tripping" in Bethel's fields was the future of our nation and world protesting a killing field in Viet Nam, which in 1968 was the bloodiest year of that war. Thousands of beautiful, promising young people were gone. Former Nixon White House aid and presidential candidate, Pat Buchanan, believes 1968 to be the worst, most divisive, year in American history.

Attempting to seek protection from the lightning and wind at Woodstock was a young generation experiencing the widest generation gap in history, the August 1968 Democratic National Convention riots in Chicago, and the onset of the women's rights movement (which protested the Miss American Pageant in Atlantic City).

On Bethel's pastureland was a generation raised on the philosophy of Dr. Benjamin Spock, vacillating between the darker side and brighter side of humanity, and celebrating the music of *Hair*, which gave a Broadway blessing to the dramatic change in music our culture had experienced.

To say there was a great divide between the victorious generation of WWII and the V-finger victory sign wavers exhibited by their post-WWII children is putting it mildly. By 1969 our nation was on a mad dash, to who knew where, that soon produced the first resignation of a president and placed in the White House the first person not elected to either the office of vice president or president.

Other than the birth of my third daughter, about the only good thing I can remember about 1969 occurred a month before Woodstock when two American astronauts walked on the moon for the first time and took, as Neal Armstrong put it, "...one small step for man and one giant leap for mankind." From that moment on, Joseph

Campbell reminds us, we stopped talking about the "Man in the Moon" and talked of men on the moon. For good or ill, the times had changed forever and would and will never be the same again regardless of how hard we try to make them the same again politically, socially, economically, or religiously.

Not to be trite, but Woodstock was the best of times and the worst of times. But, what a time it was. My Bulova reminds me of this each time I wind it up, each time it starts to tick, and each time I wear it to a special event, which is the only time I place it on my left wrist. That's chronos time.

Kairos Time

The second Greek word for time is *kairos.*

Kairos is the word Jesus often used when he referred to time. We don't have a word in our language that comes from the Greek kairos. Kairos means special time, the right time, the opportune or supreme moment, in the fullness of time. Kairos is a time in which your whole life is caught up in the moment, everything crystallizes, and everything hinges on whether you say "yes" or "no." It is a time when you decide to follow your bliss or ignore it. It is one of those "Ah" experiences, not too frequently encountered in life, but when it happens, you know something extraordinary has occurred.

For me, Bethel's Woodstock was not only a chronos time, it was also a Kairos time. Some may deny that and that's OK. I will never deny it. Having lived there for over three days, I affirm the Kairos Time I encountered there. I affirm it still. I affirm it as a pastor, student of the Bible, from my understanding of Biblical theology, my studies of the mythology of many cultures, and from my seven-plus decades of living. Woodstock was a kairos opportune, supreme moment time.

For good or ill, I knew these three days of peace and music as a kairos moment, a special time, where life for many was caught up in a great moment and movement, everything crystallized and hinged on whether those attending, or attempting to, could give their "yes" or "no" to the experience of living they were having. We lived those three days in the fullness of time, Kairos Time.

Vision

Music and poetry, indeed all the arts, reflect where a people or a society are at any given time. The arts help us define what we think, believe, dream, hope, and understand about life. The arts are the reflecting glass showing us who and were we are as a culture. The arts are the mirrors into which we look to see where we have been and what culture looks like, thinks, hopes, and dreams. The arts give us vision. Bethel's Woodstock was a vision quest. Through music and its poetry, a vision of life was projected.

The Woodstock generation, which came from all over the globe, were on a vision quest. They came looking for a life of meaning, searching for a reason for being alive in the tornadic closing years of the '60s. I don't believe the vision was fully achieved. Most usually are not. Some are, partially. As Mike Wright states in *What They Didn't Tell You About the 60s:*

> *For many in America, the 1960's were magical times—times for coming of age and times for coming apart. Much has changed since the sixties-- much in America, the world, and in us.*
>
> *We like to visit the sixties, at least visit words and pictures and memories of the time. In the sixties, America grew up.* (p. 341.)

Yes, America grew up in the '60s, and we left behind much of the vision we sought. Unfortunately, we didn't have a dream catcher, as the Native Americans call it, to snare the positive vision and let the negative slip through, doing no harm. I think many missed carrying that vision, which gives meaning to being alive, into the future. Most of those at Woodstock grew up, got married, had children, and were shaped by the times and circumstances, not only of the '60s but also of the '70s and '80s. The vision so earnestly sought on Bethel's hill in 1969 remains illusive. And there is a catch-22, a dichotomy to it, as there is with most of life. It is not a black or white thing. Neither is life good or bad. There is a yin and yang to it.

Take my brother, for example. At nineteen, in the year of Woodstock, he wanted to blow up the smoke stacks of the Otis Elevator Company in Yonkers, New York, because they represented the "gone wrong" society he protested. Yet, Otis was where our father, one of the greats in the greatest generation, worked during WWII, making aircraft carrier elevator lifts in the effort to defeat Nazism and Imperial Japan. Otis Elevator put food on our table, clothes on our back, and eventually a college education for three and a nursing RN for another. The polluting smoke stacks provided for us and gave us the right to protest the society in which we lived. It was, and still is, like being between a rock and a hard place.

Who was right? Who was wrong?

It's not a matter of right or wrong. It's a matter of where you jump into the fray. The battle, for an experience of being alive and the quest for a life of meaning, is one into which we are all invited. It is not a private fight; it is a public fight. And when we join in, we help perpetuate the yin and yang of life. We keep the vision of hope alive.

Today my brother, a grandfather, owns a nice home, boat, and cars in Maine where he spent his working years in the state's juvenile justice system.

Where did his vision go?

I know, from our conversations, that his vision remained alive in his work with the youth of Maine who fell into trouble with the law. Is it still there for those who made it to Bethel or wanted to? Are we beginning to see it come into focus with the election of our first African-American president? I don't know. I live in hope. I live with a vision. And I hope for the thousands who sought that vision in Bethel in music, art, unity, peace, and love that it is still alive. Why? Because "where there is no vision the people perish." (Proverbs 29:18 KJV)

There is another side to vision, or lack of it. While I was but a stone's throw from the stage, I only saw it when away from our trailer. More often than not, it was out of my vision. I could not see the performers. I heard them, yes, but could not bring most of them into my vision. However, because I couldn't see all of them didn't mean they were not real or not there. Their sounds were there. There voices were there. Their words were there. I had a vision in my mind's eye of what was transpiring on that stage. But years later, when I saw all the musical giants on that stage, via film and video, I caught a vision of Woodstock I had only heard.

Putting words with persons makes a difference in what one sees and understands, visions and knows. When the unseen becomes the seen, our vision, both mythically and physically, is different. Seeing, via video and film, the passion, hope, sincerity, and vision of the performers, as they stood before five hundred thousand people, helped me catch the vision of Woodstock and gave me a new appreciation for the proverb, "where there is no vision the people perish."

Myth

For many, myth is that which is false, fairy tale stories, and the untrue. I do not view myth that way. I do not understand myth as something primitive or, by definition, false or superstitious. Humankind has always depended upon significant myths to bring meaning to life. Without a proper myth-system, humanity is in trouble: vision blurs and perishes, and life becomes devoid of meaning. We all live our lives out of myths whether we admit it or not. We may not call them myths, but they are. Myths bring meaning to our lives. That which gives our lives meaning may be money, sports, sex, entertainment, drugs, religion, gambling, alcohol—you name it. Whatever it is that makes our lives go round and gives us reason for getting up in the morning is our myth.

However, a proper myth gives one more than that. A significant myth gives us a life with meaning. A viable myth enables us to experience being alive. In many ways we live with outdated, shallow, and meaningless myths today. Many contemporary myths are no longer helpful to life. We have not redefined or recreated myths to fit our twenty-first-century world. As Joseph Campbell, states, "The heliocentric universe has never been translated into a mythology. Science and religion have therewith gone apart." (Joseph Campbell, *The Inner Reaches of Outer Space, Metaphor as Myth and as Religion*, Harper & Row, Publishers, Inc. New York: 1986, p. 43.)

Science, through theory and experiment, takes us outward to the experience of knowledge by asking questions like: what, how, when (and some scientists are now beginning to ask, who).

Religion, through its myths, should take us inward to the experience of being alive, to discovering a life of meaning by asking questions like: what, how, who, why.

What Are Myths?

Myths, properly defined, are a set of stories or ideas that try to make sense out of the world and our place in it. Myths, as Joseph Campbell and others suggest, are big ideas that make a person think about what it means to be alive. All religious experiences may be explored as myths and interpreted as myths. This includes the Judeo-Christian-Islamic experience. This great religious tradition has been hesitant to explore its great faith stories mythologically because of the historical nature of this religious experience and our misunderstandings of what myths are. Where did we ever get the notion that to do so is wrong? There is nothing wrong with interpreting our religious experiences mythologically. Indeed by not doing so, we miss the whole point of some of our greatest religious motifs.

Unlike the religions of the Eastern world, Hinduism, Jainism, Buddhism, etc., those of the Judeo-Christian-Islamic Western tradition have understood Abraham, Moses, David, the prophets, Jesus, Paul, Mohammed, etc. mostly as historical figures. Indeed they are, or may be, but we must not let that blind us to the myths inherent in these historical religious figures. The myths surrounding them can give meaningful interpretation to all ages, including ours. The religions of the East have had no problem experiencing the myths in their faith experience. For further exploration of this, I recommend Joseph Campbell's book *Thou Art That, Transforming Religious Metaphor* as a great resource.

Question: How do we deal historically with the ascension of Jesus, or Elijah or Mohammed? Take, for example, the ascension of Jesus as merely historical. If this event is only historical, then we must admit from our twenty-first-century understanding of cosmology that Jesus, ascending at the speed of light, has not yet left our galaxy.

Further, what about heaven itself? Is heaven up there? Again, our twenty-first-century cosmologically informs us that we cannot support that concept anymore.

However, we can support these mysterious components of life and faith from a mythological perspective. To repeat, myths take us inward to the experience of being alive.

Speaking as a Christian, because that is where I am most comfortable, the transfiguration, resurrection, and ascension of Jesus go far beyond the historical. They are not only things that happened to Jesus back then, they are also meant to speak to you, me, our world, universe, and culture now. The myth surrounding these events informs us that the transfiguration, resurrection, and ascension were not only a Jesus event, they are also a you and me event. Jesus's transfiguration is transfiguration for you and me. His resurrection is resurrection for you and me. His ascension is ascension for you and me.

Mythologically, the great mysteries of life and faith should provoke us to look into our own inner space, our inner being, to life's core. As we do, we find ourselves asking key life-informing questions, such as:

What do these mysteries of life and faith inform me about my life and world?

How do I assimilate them and use them to give meaning to my being and culture?

Who is speaking in and through these experiences?

Why should these mysteries of life and faith be meaningful to my life and the world?

I have a cousin who is active in his church, sings in the choir. He owns a restaurant. Each Thanksgiving he asks his priest how many families in the parish could use a Thanksgiving meal. He then gives the priest vouchers to his restaurant. Any family coming to his establishment with one of these vouchers receives a free meal. He also does this with veterans and anyone who asks him for a meal.

When I asked him why he did this, his response demonstrated that the myth surrounding his faith became an inner experience allowing him to experience being alive by discovering a life of meaning. His faith, somewhere along his life's journey, provoked him to explore the mysteries of life and faith. He looked into his own inner being, to his life's core, and he asked and answered, for himself: what, how, who, why? His experiences in worship and church moved from an external experience to an internal one. Thus he put words into action. Ideas into practice.

In my Christian tradition, St. Paul, writing to the church at Galatia, remarks, "...it is no longer I who live, but it is Christ who lives in me." (Galatians 2:20 NRSV)

Christ, for Paul, was more than an historical figure, he was eternal, mythological. Paul allowed this Christ to become apart of his inner being in such a powerful way that Paul sensed Christ living in him. In another of his letters, Paul writes to the Philippians, "...for me to live is Christ." (Philippians 1:21 NRSV)

This is what myths are intended to do.

Proper myths have a mystical function in relation to life. The words myth *mythos*), mystic (*mystikos*), and mystery (*myst + erion*) come from the same common root word. All carry us beyond our world and our self into the mystical and mysterious.

Myths help us make sense out of our ever-changing mysterious culture, world, universe, and cosmology. Our culture, world, universe, and cosmology should complement our myths, and our myths should complement our culture, world, universe, and cosmology.

Unfortunately, we do not allow this to happen because we are hung up on the history connected with our myths and not the mystery inherent in them. Thus, we find it nearly impossible to allow the myths, which permeate our Judeo-Christian-Islamic tradition, to open us to the mysterious consciousness that is all around us.

Myths are intended to help us understand our social order and our society. Properly understood, they enable us to see how we fit in to all that surrounds us. The myths in our Western religions should inform us of who we are in the world. They should help us navigate through the great stages and passages of life: birth, childhood, adulthood, aging, death, and beyond.

The proper function of myths then is to place us in harmony with our often confusing and mysterious culture, world, universe, and cosmology.

Woodstock as Myth

What has all this to do with Woodstock's Bethel?

For me, it has everything to do with it.

Among many at Bethel, there was an underlying, maybe unconscious, search for harmony with the confusing and mysterious culture, world, universe, and cosmology they knew. There seemed to be a search for a myth that might open them to the experience of being alive and make sense out of their (our) culture, world, universe, and cosmology. In my opinion, the drugs, music, dress, free love, and hippie lifestyle expressed at

Bethel were outward signs of a quest for a much deeper, inward, life-defining myth that would place them in harmony with the world in which they lived, moved, and experienced their being.

This quest was not fully realized or discovered. It seldom is. Long after the last song was sung at Woodstock, the search remained. The struggle to discover a myth which can give meaning to life still goes on in the twenty-first century. Fortunately it does go on because in that quest is humankind's hope for the future. Will we ever find a meaningful myth for our age? Or will we be forever on the quest?

One cannot predict the next mythology any more than one can predict tonight's dream; for a mythology is not an ideology. It is not something projected from the brain, but something experienced from the heart, from recognitions of identities behind or within the appearances of nature, perceiving with love a "thou" where there would have been otherwise only an "it." As stated already centuries ago in the Indian Kena Upanishad [29]: "That which in the lightning flashes forth, makes one blink, and say 'Ah!'—that 'Ah!' refers to divinity."

... or as a setting sun ignites the sky, or a deer seen standing alerted, the exclamation "Ah!" may

be uttered as a recognition of divinity." (Campbell, 1986,. 18–19.)

It behooves us to discover, or rediscover, that God's revelation to us is that which speaks "Ah!" or "Awe" to you. It could be a flower, sky, art, dance, mountain, music, Yahweh, Buddha, Jesus, God, Allah, Mohamed, etc.

There were signs of an "Ah!" or "Awe" at Woodstock, a mythology wanting to be born from the collective heart of those gathered. We lived life in the "Awe" and "Ah" of the moment. There was an I and Thou spirit that permeated the scene. There was a fleeting recognition of divinity there. For me Bethel was a potential myth-shaper event. Those there were one with Bethel and were one with Woodstock. They were Bethel. They were Woodstock. The journey walked in Bethel was a mysterious and mythical search journey. For three days the center of the universe was in that place and the universe was centered there. There were no "its" or "them." It was us, I, and Thou.

My senses told me that the mud/earth walked by those there gave a sense of being; it was as if we were being re-created from the ground. There was a oneness with the muddy earth, and it was one with us. In some ways it was the "ground" of our being. We were like Adam, "Man of the Red Earth." The formless void of flock pasture of Max Yatsgur's dairy farm became a living, breathing organism of humankind centered in the mythological, almost divine, music, poetry, and art all around us. Life was born there, three died there, people were hungry there, people were fed there, and others were injured or ill there and were cared for there.

I cannot forget the wind brought by thunderstorms. It was like the breath of God. *Ruah* in Hebrew means breath or spirit. Bethel's Ruah was breathed into our communal nostrils, giving life and threatening life at once. The breath of life filling our common lungs made us a living organism.

My ears still hear the crisp, sharp lightning bolts slicing through the heavy air, shattering the darkness and piercing ears with the thunder that followed. Ground shook. Bones shook. It was like a baptism by fire. Lightning has often been viewed as a symbol of religious fervor and martyrdom. In mythology, the lightning flash often symbolizes enlightenment. Woodstock was an enlightening experience opening to me new understandings and an appreciation for what had been foreign to me.

Dark, threatening clouds hung menacingly overhead like a heavy veil. One mythical understanding of clouds is that they symbolize the unseen, that which veils humankind or hides us from God or heaven. Much was clouded at Woodstock, much not understood, much not seen. Deep within me, to this hour, there is a somewhat veiled mystery about that Bethel experience.

The drenching August rains cascaded down like water over a waterfall. I sensed it as a kind of baptism. In baptism it is water, living water, that cleanses, washes away, and gives life. In more than one way, Woodstock was a cleansing for me, washing away many of my preconceived prejudices about the "Sixties Generation."

The food shared was like the feeding of the five thousand on a hillside near Bethsaida (house of fishing) and the Sea of Galilee where a lad had five loaves and two fishes. When shared, the multitude was fed with fragments leftover. Give me bread to eat. And bread was given by the gentle, peace-loving Hog Farm and those who had brought provisions, area church groups, other local residents, and organizations. I saw people being fed wherever I visited. It was a movable feast. No one went hungry, and no one was overfed.

The helicopters were like Jacob's ladder. They descended and ascended, their blades cutting through the thick soupy air as they carried the musical deities who performed on the Woodstock stage. The godlike superstars descended to earth proclaiming their messages of peace, love, and hope to their worshipers, then ascended into the heavens, leaving the faithful waiting for the next "angelic" visitor.

Woodstock was an "Awe" happening. It was an "Ah!" experience, an awesome place. It was Bethel. The journey we walked was a mysterious, mythical, search journey.

Metaphor

We moderns have a world view that I believe is one of the major causes of some of our greatest problems. We see everything as fact, figures, definable, analytical, scientific, political, digital, economic, military, historical, the bottom line, etc. Through this world view, we live our lives and search for a life of meaning. We have cast in stone this way of thinking and, as a result, have cast off another way of thinking which for me is just as real.

I refer here to metaphor.

We have all but eliminated a metaphorical view of life. As a human being, and as a pastor, my world view has always included seeing things not only from the factual, scientific, analytical, historical perspective but also from a metaphoric perspective. For me a coin has two sides. There is always a plus and minus: the positive and negative, the yin and yang, that prevent our universe from flying apart into billions and billions of particles.

Metaphors are comparisons showing how two things that are not alike in most ways are similar in one important way. Metaphors are a way to describe something. Unlike similes that use the words "as" or "like" to make a comparison, metaphors state that something *is* something else.

The Beth-el of the Bible *is* the Bethel of Woodstock. That's the metaphor.

I had a seminary professor who began each lecture with a Biblical joke, a brainteaser, or riddle. One day he walked into class, put his notes on the lectern, and said, "Let us pray." He finished the prayer, said "Amen," and asked, "Which came first, the chicken or the egg?" After an appropriate pause, he answered, "They both came at the same time—one inside the other." With that the lecture began, and no more was said.

I have mused over that class opener ever since. It makes sense, yet it makes no sense. It is simplistic, yet profound. It is true, yet false. It is religious, yet mythological. It is fact, yet metaphorical. The egg is the chicken, and the chicken is the egg. There is the metaphor.

Which came first, Beth-el of the Bible or Bethel of Woodstock? They both came at the same time, one inside the other. The Beth-el of the Bible is the Bethel of Woodstock. There is the metaphor.

As recorded in Genesis 28:10-22, Jacob had a dream.

What a dream it was.

He slept with his head on a rock for a pillow. The dream that ensued put him between a rock and a hard place. He saw "...a ladder set up on the earth, the top of it reaching to heaven." He envisioned "...angels of God... ascending and descending on [the ladder]."

This is nothing less than two-way communication. Communication between God's angels (in Greek, *angelos* means messenger) and Jacob.

The Lord stood beside him and spoke to him a promise. This promise was not new; it had been made to

Jacob's parents, Isaac and Rebekah, and to his grandparents, Abraham and Sarah. It was a promise of land and a family too large to number that would bless all the families of earth. The promise also stated, "Know that I am with you and will keep you wherever you go, and will bring you back to this land; for I will not leave you until I have done what I have promised you."

Jacob awoke and exclaimed, "How awesome is this place! This is none other than the house of God, and this is the gate of heaven...He called that place Beth-el."

The metaphor: "This *is*...the house of God...*is* the gate of heaven."

He took his stone pillow, poured oil on it, made a vow and proclaimed, "...this stone, which I have set up for a pillar, shall be God's house [Beth-el]..."

The metaphor: "...this stone...shall be [*is*] God's house."

Returning to the apostle Paul, is there metaphor in his words we quoted earlier, "...it is no longer I who live, but it *is* Christ who lives in me," and, "...for me, to live *is* Christ...?" Personally, I think so. Life, to the apostle, *is* Christ who gave Paul a life of meaning, the full experience of being alive.

Metaphor. We have lost metaphor. We are practical, scientific, logical. We live with prose and not poetry. We have lost metaphor in our lives.

Metaphor Lost in Time

What are we to make of Jacob's awesome place? What are we to make of this gate of heaven? What are we to make of the house of God?

Maybe the more appropriate question is: What have we made of them? And perhaps: What have we refused to make of them?

What we have done is take the metaphor out of these places. We have refused to allow them to speak to us metaphorically. We have lost the metaphor inherent in them. Metaphor has been lost in time.

In so doing, we have made these places what they were never intended to be. Instead we have made these places: chaos, hunger, anger, conflict, hatred, war, death, despair. To this day the physical, geographical, actual awesome place—house of God, gate of heaven—is in blood-filled turmoil as it has been for centuries. Yet, by finding again the metaphor in these places we can see them for what they have always been intended.

At one time gods were tied to the land in which they were worshiped. In conquest of a land, the natives would often be punished by exile. To be exiled is to be banished from one's home, cut off from one's god. In Latin, the word *exilium* comes from *ex,* meaning *out,* and *solium,* meaning *ground.* To force a people into exile is to take them away from their land, where their gods dwelt, and place them in a strange land of other gods. To the exiled people, their deities were no more because they were back in a land where there was no one to worship them. In a very real sense, their deities were dead. A god without worshipers is no god.

Exile was the fate of the kingdom of Judah. Judah was conquered by the Babylonians and carried off into exile in Babylon for nearly fifty years (586 to 537 BCE). A major lesson was learned there, thanks to the prophets of the exile like Jeremiah, Ezekiel, Daniel and the like. The lesson learned was that the God of Jacob's dream and promise, the God of Beth-el, the God of the gate of heaven, was not confined to the land, was not fixed in stone in a geographic place. The God the people of Judah thought they left behind in the land of Jacob's dream and promise, the God of Beth-el, was bigger and beyond that, was alive and well in their exiled and post-exiled lives.

But we like to keep our god(s) under our control, confined to the boundaries we create. We do not see the metaphor, only the factual, historical. We just can't give up our landlocked god(s), confined to history, chronological chronos.

Is the land of Jacob's dream and promise just a place, or is it also a metaphor? How we answer makes a cosmic difference. In our current era, we have answered by viewing it only as a geographic and historic place. We have failed to see it as a metaphor. The metaphor was lost.

I believe we do the same with the Bethel of Woodstock. To most it was (and is) only a place on the map of Sullivan County where something historic happened in 1969 and where, today, there is a historical marker, museum, and performing arts center. To me Woodstock is more than that. It is also a metaphor. Joseph Campbell suggests that we leave ourselves with a major problem when we see only fact and fail to see the metaphor in stories such as Jacob's Beth-el and the Bethel of Woodstock.

In the popular nightmare of history, where local mythic images are interpreted, not as metaphor, but as facts, there have been ferocious wars waged between the parties of such contrary manners of metaphoric representation. The Bible abounds in examples. And today, in the formerly charming little city of Beirut, the contending zealots of three differing inflections even of the same idea of a single paternal "God" are unloading bombs on each other. (Campbell, 1986, p. 58.)

Please note well that that those words were copywrited in 1986. We are now in the twenty-first century and still unload bombs on each other in the land where Beth-el is located. And we do so, in part, because the metaphor is lost.

However, when we go beyond what we say is only fact and permit metaphor to also inform us about such things as Jacob's dream of land and promise, and the Woodstock event in Bethel, New York, a very different image manifests itself:

The Old Testament motif of the Promised Land, interpreted comparatively [as metaphor], ...takes on a meaning very different from that of a divine mandate to conquer and occupy by military force an already populated area of the Near East...The Promised Land, therefore, is any landscape recognized as mythologically transparent, and the method of acquisition of such a territory is not by prosaic physical action, but poetically, by intelligence and the method of art; so that the human being should be dwelling in the two worlds simultaneously of illuminated moon and illuminating sun. (Campbell, 1986, p. 61–62)

Jacob said: "Surely the LORD is in this place—and I did not know it!" And he was afraid, and said, "How awesome is this place! This is none other than the house of God [Beth-el] and this is the gate of heaven."

Where is this Awesome Place in which was the Lord? Where is this House of God? Where is this Gate of Heaven?

I am writing this part of the book at my daughter and grandson's apartment in Arizona. This is Navajo country. "The Navaho of the North American Southwest identify every feature of their mythology: the coyotes, the various mountains, water-courses, frogs, serpents, rainbows, spiders, red ants, dragonflies, and so on—so that wherever they go and whatever they see, they are in mind of supporting powers." (Campbell, 1986, p. 61.)

We have supporting powers too. All we need do to experience our supporting powers is to allow the metaphors in the great motifs of our Judeo-Christian-Islamic faith to reach out and speak to us. Buddhism, Hinduism, Jainism, and other Eastern religions have always done this. Allowing our great religious traditions to speak to us as metaphors enables us to embark on the quest, the journey of discovering that Awesome Place in which the Lord is; the place where the House of God (the Beth-el of the Bible and the Bethel of Woodstock) is; the location of the Gate of Heaven is found wherever we go and in whatever we see.

The Beth-el of the Bible is the Bethel of Woodstock.

Bethel's Woodstock is a historical place, yes, but for me it is also a metaphor, a state of mind, a place of being. It was an awesome place, an awesome experience. It was Bethel. The journey I walked in Bethel in 1969 was both a mythical search journey and a metaphor. I had that same experience forty years later.

Bethel Time:
June 2009 to June 2010

In June of 2009, I e-mailed a rough first draft of this book to the Museum at Bethel Woods to see if they would be interested in publishing it. I discovered that they do not publish material but would be interested in having it in their gift shop. However, they did express great interest in my staff badge and wondered if I would donate it to the museum for display in their upcoming 2010 "Collecting Woodstock Exhibit."

When I heard the words "donate it," it was like being asked to donate my firstborn. On second thought, that might have been easier. Donate it? I had to mull that one over for a while. It turned out to be a twelve-month mull.

With much angst, I contacted the museum and agreed to give the badge to their permanent collection. Carolee and I planned the drive to the museum on Saturday, June 26, 2010. Early that morning, I programmed our Garmin for 200 Hurd Road, Bethel, New York 12720. We were on the road by 10:15 a.m. in our two-week-old Prius Hybrid. Think Green! Yes, Woodstock helped me do that.

The last time I was at the festival site was a month or two after the tenth anniversary in 1979. There was nothing there then but a marker. I was a bit nostalgic about this trip. I had no idea what awaited me.

The weather was warm and sunny; it was a delightful day for an early summer drive. We entered the Garden State Parkway North at Clifton, paid our E-ZPass tolls, and exited onto New Jersey Route 17 North, at Paramus. Up to the New York State Thruway we rolled, entering at interchange 15, Suffern, and exiting at interchange 16, Harriman. We were now on the route to Bethel, New York, 17 North, the Quickway. We were getting fifty miles to the gallon and making great time. Tires clickity-clacked, thump-thumped over the road seams up Route 17 for about ten minutes at sixty MPH.

Then, everything came to a sudden halt. It was bumper to bumper, headlight to taillight. We sat and waited. Waited and sat. Some turned off their engines. Others got out of their cars, strolled around, walked their dogs, sat on the guardrails; still other had to seek relief in the roadside bushes. It was a parking lot.

My mind was at once thrown back to my, pre-gas crisis, 1968 blue Chevelle on my way to Woodstock, and no longer in the 2010 fifty-MPG Prius on the way to Woodstock. As Yogi Berra, whose grandchildren I baptized, once said, "It was déjà vu all over again." I heard Rod Serling's voice, "You have entered the Twilight Zone." It was a space-time continuum. It was a flashback re-creation of August '69. At least all of this ran through my mind as we sat for forty minutes until traffic started to move again.

After a ten-minute twenty-MPH drive, we saw that the delay was caused by a travel trailer accident. The RV was torn apart and scattered all over the median strip. An overturned pickup truck was near it. Our prayer was that no one was seriously, hurt but there were fire equipment, police cruisers, and ambulances all around the horrific scene.

We continued on the Quickway to exit 104 and onto Route 17 B. It would be a ten-mile drive to Bethel. As the clock was now approaching noon, we were yearning for some grub. We whizzed past a place called Bubba's Barbeque. Carolee said, "Turn around, go back. That looks nice."

Nice? As we were to soon discover, it was more than nice. The view overlooked serene, beautiful White Lake. We ordered and had some iced tea while waiting. Soon our order was up. We had pulled pork sandwiches with onion rings served by a most welcoming wait staff. It was the best pulled pork I had had since a trip to Charlotte, North Carolina, on church business. Bubba's slogan is, "Put a Little South in Your Mouth." Yes, we did, thank you very much!

After a visit to the restrooms, to wash our heavenly greasy paws, we forced our now overly stuffed selves into the Prius and drove the few miles to Hurd Road. Down a beautifully landscaped road to a paved parking lot we rolled. I didn't remember paved parking lots back in 1969, just grassy, dusty pasture temporarily loaned for use as a parking lot by Gus Yatsgur. It was quite nice. As we traversed the path to the museum entrance, I noticed that the place was immaculately clean—a far cry from my first visit.

I was back in 1969 again, recalling that hot day, the smell of brown, dry hay underfoot the first time I traversed these coordinates. The multitudes were again stretched out before my mind's eye. The promenade I was taking now was not too far from the beaten path I strolled the first time I walked on this mystical, awesome ground. My Bulova watch was on my left wrist; my staff badge was in a plastic sandwich bag in my shirt pocket. I was deeply aware of both. The watch seemed to tighten its Speidel band on my arm. I felt the badge's corner poking my chest, and I envisioned when I first wore it for real those many years ago.

The entrance gate to the museum walk was in front of us. The sign naming the site was in the center of the entrance. Carolee said, "Come on, let me get your picture."

As she prepared to shoot me (there are times she really would like to), a couple came up and said, "Peace! Is this your first time here?"

I replied, "No, not for me, for my wife, yes. I was here in 1969 and have come to donate my staff badge to the museum."

"Staff badge?"

"Yes, I was a chaplain at the original Woodstock."

This always gets folks interested. Why a chaplain at Woodstock? What did you do as a pastor at Woodstock? What was it really like? How did you get the job? Q and A session over, our newfound Woodstock friends took our picture in front of the sign. I showed them my badge and watch. Off they went as we continued on into the museum.

A volunteer at the information booth greeted us. I explained we had an appointment with Robin Green, executive assistant. "She's expecting you; I'll give her a call and let her know you're here." Robin would be with us shortly.

Not only did Robin greet us, she brought the museum director, Wade Lawrence, as well. We were invited downstairs to the executive office suites.

Once in the administrative offices, I presented my badge, which, as I said, was professionally secured in a plastic sandwich bag. After some conversation and reminiscing, I filled out the proper legal donation forms required by the museum. White gloves were used to remove the badge from the sandwich bag. It was carefully placed on a table, photos of the badge were taken, others of the badge with Carolee and me were taken. With white gloves on, Wade slipped the badge in a more secure folder. He said I would be contacted to share information on my presentation for the information plate that would be next to the badge. I asked for a membership form, and we became supporting members of The Museum at Bethel Woods.

We went upstairs for a complimentary tour of the museum. I was moved by the professional quality of the displays. Upon entering, one is introduced to the museum with quotes and clips from some of those who performed at Woodstock. A most wonderful display reflects the 1960s in pictures, capturing it much like Mike Wright does in his book, *What They Didn't Teach You About the 60s*, and especially the Chronology he so aptly reports. Visitors are then introduced to the planning and creation of what became Woodstock and the experience attendees had in getting to the event itself. All this is depicted as you sit in a psychedelically painted school bus where a film describes the Woodstock experience. A multimedia production explores the festival site via a touch screen interactive program. I found it difficult to operate, but those around me, who were much younger, had not a problem. Finally, through the displays, one gets to explore the 1960s and the impact that decade had on the present day.

There is an unwritten law Carolee and I have about visiting museums. We never go to a museum without exiting through the gift shop where it is required that something is purchased. The requirement is Carolee's, not mine. However, this time I found a book I wanted to have, so she purchased it. The book is: *Woodstock '69: Three Days of Peace, Music & Medical Care,* by Myron Gittell, RN, with Jack Kelly, EMT. It is a fascinating account of Woodstock from the perspective of the medical care needed at the festival.

Book and two posters in hand, we stopped at the snack bar. I believe this is another unwritten law Carolee has when it comes to visiting museums. Well, it's mine too. We ordered coffee for Carolee and a bottle of healthy spring water for me.

Fully refreshed, we drove down Hurd Road to West Shore Road where Robin Green had told us the original marker commemorating this world event is located. We parked in the small parking lot and walked to the monument. I stood there in silence and read the words on the marker:

THIS IS THE ORIGINAL SITE

OF THE

WOODSTOCK

MUSICAL AND ARTS FAIR

HELD ON AUG. 15, 16, 17, 1969

My eyes rose up from the monument, and into vision came the area where the stage had been all those decades ago, about two hundred yards away. Not far from there had been the trailer out of which I worked. It was like one of those movie melts where the current scene fades into a past scene on the same site. I could see the stage, the crowds. I could hear the music, the noise. I could smell the damp, wet, mud, and marijuana-infused air. I could feel those three days of peace and music flowing through my veins of memory. I was back in a mystical, magical place.

I don't know how long I stood looking at the stage area and the hillside once filled with thousands, but I was abruptly brought back to the present by a young woman (about twenty), standing near the monument with a friend. She was taking photos with her digital camera. As she peered through the view finder taking other pictures, she said to her companion, "My folks always said I was a hippie. I'd give anything to have been here."

I turned to her and said, "I was here, and I am here still."

"What do you mean?" she asked.

I told her about my work there as a chaplain and some of my memories of the site and the event. Then I said, "Woodstock is forever. It is ingrained in my very being. The summer of 1969 ended a horrible decade and ushered in all that happened since. In some significant way, all the changes in racism, class and gender struggles, sexism, sexual orientation, and the like were pushed to the forefront partially because of the three days of peace and music experienced on the very spot on which we stand. I was here. I am here."

We returned to the Prius. Carolee drove down West Shore Road. There was a pullout area behind the spot where the stage had been. Now the site is just a rise in the earth with grass growing on it. "Stop here, Carolee, I've got to see it from this perspective." We stopped and I got out of the car. My eyes looked up the grassy hillside that had served as a natural amphitheater for the audience. Inside me the hill was again filled to capacity with the faithful. I could hear the air being chopped by the helicopter blades as they descended and ascended with the gods of the music of the '60s. The landing area had not been too far from where I was now standing.

I got back in the car. Tears ran down my cheeks. Why? I don't know. Maybe it was because I had returned to a very special, mystical, metaphorical place. Carolee drove down West Shore Road back to 17B, turned left, headed toward the Quick Way, the New York State Thruway, and home. We pulled into our driveway in Montclair, New Jersey, an hour and a half later. What a day it had been. I would be back on some tomorrow.

Tomorrow

When is it tomorrow?

Some suggest tomorrow never comes. The moment we think it is tomorrow, it is the present. The moment we think we have grasped today, it is yesterday.

Yesterday; today; tomorrow. Past; present; future. If we own any of those three, it is probably today, the present. Once today or the present becomes yesterday or tomorrow, it is gone and cannot be retrieved. Once tomorrow or the future becomes today or the present, we realize how fleeting time is and how difficult it is to fully grasp.

So tomorrow I will open my dresser drawer, see my Bulova watch there, but the badge will not be in the cozy corner of the upper drawer housing my white tube socks and hankies. It will be at the Museum at Bethel Woods. It will be there for tomorrows to come for all who come in the present and see it and for all those who saw it in the past.

But the watch remains with me and will be wound and worn on special occasions. That watch symbolizes a time when for three days peace and music hovered over a steamy, wet, noisy place called Bethel. Or was it Beth-el? It was there where I lived and shared with thousands a most awesome time. Woodstock is and will forever be fused deeply in my inner core. Woodstock was a time when for a brief, fleeting moment, hope for a better world permeated the air. Looking back over the years, I am still amazed at how it shaped and changed my life.

It was in no way a perfect time. There was an element of fear at Woodstock. Fear of the massive crowd. Fear of the weather. Fear of the unknown. Fear of a strange new paradigm and life-reforming culture hoping to be birthed.

The barrier of fear broke, and a sense of well-being and oneness came upon the mass of humanity gathered in Bethel. I have never understood fully how this occurred. It remains a mysterious part of that mythical and mysterious event. But I am often reminded of the fact that the main imperative in the Bible centers around the words: "Fear not!" "Be not afraid." Somehow we "feared not." For some reason we were not afraid.

Woodstock was, at once, a good and bad time; an easy and hard time; a yin and yang time. But isn't that true of all life? What is good? What is bad? What is an easy time? What is a hard time? What is right? What is wrong?

It is not a matter of either or, it is a matter of both at once. As suggested earlier, what is good for some is bad for others. What is an easy time for others, is a hard time for some. What is right for one, is wrong for others.

In the USA's Civil War, or if you prefer, the War Between the States, the North thought they were right and the South wrong. The Southerners were equally convinced they were right and the Yankees were wrong. Both sides knew for sure that God was on their side and invoked God's help. Why?

Adolph Hitler, and the hoards who followed him, thought they were right. Why? I don't know. But they really believed he, and they, were right. Those opposed to Nazism thought they were right and it was wrong. Why?

The segregationists of the Old South thought they were right and integration was wrong. Those in the civil rights movement thought their cause right and the segregationists were wrong. Why?

It all depends on from where you are coming.

Life is not a matter of right and wrong. It is a struggle, a battle, a fray. Life is a public, not a private, fight into which anyone can jump. The point is, we must jump in somewhere. A person jumps into the fray from his or her life-shaping experiences: culture, education, history, religion, heritage. These shape our decision-making process in relation to right and wrong in our struggle for a life of meaning and the experience of being truly alive.

This is true of the Woodstock experience as well. It wasn't right or wrong, good or bad. It was a happening, a quest for a life of meaning, an experience of being alive.

We all jumped into the battle from our many varied backgrounds and conquered the initial barrier of fear. Into the fray we jumped, fought, learned, grew, struggled, shared our bread and drink, laughed, cried, leaned on each other, survived, and moved on.

"Ah, what a time it was." My Bulova watch holds all that time in its continuing ticks and tocks. Someday I will probably think about uniting watch with badge. Someday in the fleeting future always becoming the present and past, maybe, perhaps maybe, I will donate the watch so it can go home where it was found and probably belongs.

The badge with my name on it is now in the permanent collection of the museum. Even so, it still reminds me that I was there. That badge, though no longer lodged among my socks, will always be my passport and entrance point to kairos time where for a brief moment in time I experienced a place called Bethel, or was it Beth-el, in August 1969 . Many yesterdays gone.

That badge is a also a sign of the present, of today, where I live and work and play and pray and grow older and experience a life of meaning.

Further, it is a sign of the future, tomorrow, into which I will carry my memories and experiences of the Beth-el of the Bible and the Bethel of Woodstock. It gave to many a life of meaning, an experience of being alive.

On some distant tomorrow, there will be peace and music forever. It started many yesterdays ago in locations without names. Beth-els all they are, houses of God. And where God dwells, there is no past, present, future; no yesterday, today, tomorrow. There is infinity, eternity, everlasting kairos time overflowing with hope. That hope may appear eternally impossible to attain, but on it still lives. I call it LOVE.

Being There: A Pastor at Woodstock, Then, Now, and Tomorrow

BIBLIOGRAPHY

Buber, Martin. *I and Thou*. Translated by Ronald Smith. New York: Scribner, 1937.

Brokaw, Tom. *The Greatest Generation*. New York: Random House, 1999.

Campbell, Joseph. *The Hero with A Thousand Faces*. Princeton, NJ: Princeton University Press, 1973.

Campbell, Joseph. *The Inner Reaches of Outer Space: Metaphor as Myth and as Religion*. New York: Harper & Row, Publishers, Inc., New York: 1986.

Campbell, *Joseph. Myths to Live By*. New York: Bantam Books, 1973.

Campbell, Joseph, and Bill Moyers. Edited by Betty Sue Flowers. *The Power of Myth*. New York: Doubleday, 1988. Companion to: The Video Documentary: *Joseph Campbell and the Power of Myth*. Public Broadcasting System, 1988.

Campbell, Joseph. Edited by Eugene Kennedy. *Thou Art That*. Novato, CA: New World Library, 2001.

Earisman, Delbert L. *Hippies in Our Midst*. Philadelphia: Fortress Press, 1968.

Gittel, Myron, RN with Jack Kelly, EMT. *Woodstock '69: Three Days of Peace, Music & Medical Care*. Kiamesha Lake, NY: Load N Go Press, 2009.

Holy Bible, King James Version.

Holy Bible, The New Revised Standard Version. Nashville, TN: Thomas Nelson, Inc., 1989.

Jones, Don. *Memories Poems & Essays*. Malta, NY: Open Door Publishers, Inc., 2011.

Nobel, David F. *The Religion of Technology: The Divinity of Man and The Spirit of Invention*. New York: Penguin Books, 1999.

Spock, Benjamin. *The Common Sense Book of Baby and Child Care*, rev. ed. New York: Duell, Sloan and Pearce, 1957.

Westminster Dictionary of the Bible, Philadelphia: Westminster Press, 1944.

Woodstock, 3 Days of Peace and Music, The Director's Cut, Warner Brothers, 1994

Woodstock, Music from the Original Soundtrack and More, Cottilion Records, New York, New York 1970 and Rhino Entertainment Group, Burbank, California, 2009.

Wright, Mike. *What They Didn't Teach You About the 60s*. Novato, CA: Presidio Press, Inc., 2001.

17447127R00060

Made in the USA
Lexington, KY
11 September 2012